PAINTING

DREAMS

Minnie Evans,
Visionary Artist

Mary E. Lyons

Houghton Mifflin Company   Boston 1996

To
Nina Howell Starr
and
the excellent girls and boys in
Ann J. Smith's fourth-grade class,
1993–1994,
Clark Elementary School,
Charlottesville, Virginia

Pages 2–3: *Untitled [collage of Indian and face].* Minnie's favorite paint was Venus
Oil, which she mixed with other pigments to give them a glistening shine.
18 x 14. Courtesy of Laurel Sneed.

Text copyright © 1996 by Mary E. Lyons

For information about this and other Houghton Mifflin trade and reference books and multimedia products,
visit The Bookstore at Houghton Mifflin on the World Wide Web at http://www.hmco.com/trade/.

Manufactured in the United States of America

The text of this book is set in 14/18 Dante

HOR 10 9 8 7 6 5 4 3 2 1

Library of Congress Cataloging-in-Publication Data
Lyons, Mary (Mary E.).
Painting dreams: Minnie Evans, visionary artist / Mary E. Lyons
p.   cm.
Includes bibliographical references.
Summary: A biography of the North Carolina painter whose art had its origins in her religious visions
and the African traditions of her slave ancestors.
ISBN 0-395-72032-X
1. Evans, Minnie, 1892–1982 — Juvenile literature. 2. Afro-American painters — North Carolina —
Biography — Juvenile literature. 3. Visions in art — Juvenile literature. [1. Evans, Minnie, 1892–1982.
2. Artists. 3. Afro-Americans — Biography. 4. Women — Biography.] I. Title.
ND237.E79L96 1996
760 — de20
[B] 95-3994 CIP AC

Contents

"Minnie Evans at Airlie Gate House." Courtesy of Nina Howell Starr and Photo-Researchers, New York City.

Introduction:
Inside, Outside

Minnie Evans was a traveler in a strange land. No one could journey with her to the places she visited in nightly dreams and daily visions. But midway through her life, at the age of forty-three, she became an artist. Her drawings and paintings allow the viewer to peer inside her extraordinary world.

Driven by the urge to record her dreams, Minnie created more than one thousand pieces of visionary art. She wanted to share the wisdom she found in dreams, though she believed her pictures were only imitations. "I can't paint what I dream," she said, "because my dreams are so beautiful."

There was little in Minnie's life to encourage her creative ability. Childhood friends laughed at her; teachers scolded her; and even her family doubted her sanity. Sometimes the need to draw made Minnie feel like the outsider in their world.

As an African-American living in the aftermath of slavery, Minnie also had to struggle with racism. She never admitted that prejudice bothered her. Still, it skewed the way some people viewed her art.

When she became an artist, she could not afford basic art materials and searched for throwaway pencils, crayons, and scrap paper. When Minnie ran out of paper, she used an old window shade or the cardboard cover of a worn-out book as a homemade canvas.

Deprivation and prejudice might have defeated a less spirited person. But Minnie Evans was a very determined woman. Once she decided to turn the vivid images in her head into art, nothing stood in her way.

One: A Very Peculiar Life

Minnie Evans was born Minnie Eva Jones in a log cabin in Long Creek, North Carolina, on December 12, 1892. Her mother, Ella, was just thirteen at the time. "My mother wasn't anything but a child," Minnie later remembered. When she was two months old, they moved twenty miles south to live with her grandmother, Mama Mary Croom Jones, in Wilmington, North Carolina.

Minnie's father, George Moore, was only a boy himself when she was born. Since he left town after her birth without marrying her mother, Minnie thought of herself as an "outside" child. George's family also wanted nothing to do with Minnie. They didn't bother telling her when he died during her teens. She found out by accident the year after he passed away.

If Minnie missed having a father, she never admitted it. "You know some of the men just don't want to be bothered with the outside child," she said. "It didn't worry me." She had her mother, grandmother, and great-grandmother Rachel — "my mothers, my parents"— to teach her about life.

Minnie was a solitary child who liked to draw. Her mother, Ella, encouraged her to play outside. But Minnie usually kept to herself, perhaps because she knew she was not like other girls and boys.

When she was a little girl, she heard voices call "Minnie! Minnie!" all day long. She also had waking dreams that no one else could see. These she described as "day visions," or scenes that she viewed with her eyes open.

She must have seemed odd to other children. One evening, four-year-old Minnie was playing near her house. The night was warm and the moon looked like a giant oyster shell. When she glanced up at the sky, she believed she saw elephants— one behind the other, each with its tail in the next one's mouth — marching on the ring around the moon.

"Minnie, what are you looking at?" the neighborhood children asked. Their question made her jump.

"Dream of Prophets in the Air." The fallen statues resemble those at Airlie Gardens. 11 ⅞ x 16. Courtesy of North Carolina Museum of History.

"I'm looking at those elephants going round the moon," she said.

"Minnie crazy!" they hollered. "We don't see no elephants. We don't see nothing!"

The memory of that night always saddened the artist. "I wasn't like the other children. I thought everybody could see [the animals]."

Throughout Minnie's childhood, night dreams as troubling as the day visions disturbed her sleep. Raised as a Baptist, she often dreamed about the Bible stories she heard at church. Some of these were from the books of prophets in the Old Testament.

After she fell asleep and just as the moon was setting, five or six "old Abraham prophets" appeared in her mind. She felt them carry her to the "Old Soldiers" cemetery, where Union soldiers had been buried during the Civil War. The prophets seemed to tickle her sides and toss her back and forth.

"You needn't be afraid," the old men laughed. "We ain't going to let you fall."

When Minnie cried, "I can't sleep, I can't sleep!" her grandmother put her in bed with her, and they snuggled up close until the dream went away.

Minnie's grandmother believed in supernatural events and tried to explain Minnie's experiences to her. "That's some kind of spirit that called you," Mama Mary said of the voices that her granddaughter heard all day.

Minnie, too, felt certain that the voices, visions, and dreams were what she called "natural," or real, events. "I have woke up out there [in the cemetery] more times than I can tell you," she recalled. "I've had a very peculiar life."

Mama Mary thought the dreams and voices made Minnie a special child. "Minnie," she predicted, "you gonna do something wonderful in life."

But Ella, her mother, lost patience with her. "All that sleeping and snoring you done," Ella Jones scolded in the morning, "and you telling me that you didn't rest?"

Yet dreaming left Minnie so tired that she fell asleep in school.

Perhaps she was like the composer Ludwig van Beethoven. Although he was deaf, some historians say he could hear notes being played in his head on instruments not yet invented. Minnie has also been compared to the eighteenth-century poet and artist William Blake. He claimed that he often spoke with angels and Old Testament prophets. Like these artists, Minnie Evans had visions and dreams that no one can explain.

Once she said her dreams "tormented" her. She dreamed of intricate flowers, mythical creatures, giant birds, and mysterious faces. More than a dozen times she thought she gazed upon "beautiful cities of rainbow colors."

She also saw angels, devils, and what she thought were the eyes of God. Minnie felt that the dreams gave her a secret spiritual knowledge, even as a child. "You would think that because children is children they ain't got no sense," she once said, "but children know a lot of things."

When Minnie was a child, her mother worked as a maid and as a "gatherer" who harvested oysters and clams from the sound near Wilmington, then sold them door-to-door. While Ella was at work, young Minnie

Untitled [interior scene with throw rug]. Birds, eyes, and the sun appear often in Minnie Evans's
art. 10 ¼ x 8. Courtesy of Luise Ross Gallery, New York, and the Minnie Evans Estate.

Untitled [collage of five faces]. Long eyelashes, red lips, and sweet smiles were modern symbols of feminine beauty to Minnie. Painted in twentieth-century style, these faces are a tribute to her nineteenth-century ancestral mothers. 12 x 18. Collection of the Abby Aldrich Rockefeller Folk Art Center, Williamsburg, Va. Courtesy of Luise Ross Gallery, New York, and the Minnie Evans Estate.

stayed at home with her great-grandmother Rachel and Mama Mary.

Mary was a skilled dressmaker. Freed from slavery when she was five years old, she had little opportunity to learn how to read and write. She didn't have money or fancy possessions to give as heirlooms to her granddaughter. But as Mary sewed on buttons, she told Minnie about the girl's female ancestors. These family stories were as valuable to Minnie as fine silver or old lace.

While sitting at her grandmother's knee, Minnie learned about Rachel's great-grandmother, whose name was Moni. Moni was born in Africa or was descended from an African brought to the New World as a slave.

In the late 1700s or early 1800s, she and her husband and five children were slaves on the island of Trinidad, off the northern part of South America. During that time, wealthy Spanish and French planters on Trinidad owned sugar-cane plantations run with slave labor.

At some point, the man who kept Moni and her family in slavery decided to sell them. He marched them through the mountainous jungle to the coast of the island, where slave ships waited for a full load of human cargo.

As the family trudged through the canopied rain forest, almost all of them developed deadly smallpox. According to Minnie's version of the story, Moni's husband became too sick to walk, and the slaveholder "just killed him."

Only Moni and her youngest daughter survived the disease. After they reached the coast, they were sold twice, then herded onto a boat bound for Charleston, South Carolina. The ship landed in Charleston, where Moni and her child might have been sold at a slave auction. It is not known how they reached Wilmington, North Carolina, where they were sold again on the "jailhouse block."

Nothing else is known about Rachel's great-grandmother Moni, only that she and her descendants continued to live in slavery somewhere near Wilmington.

According to Minnie, Great-Grandmother Rachel had at least twelve other children. One of them was Mama Mary. From Rachel, Mary heard the old family stories about Moni's tragic walk through the jungle and her passage to North Carolina.

Mama Mary was like an African griot, a storyteller who carefully memorizes and retells the history of his family. The stories that she heard and later retold linked Minnie to the previous generations of her family, like beads on a string. Even their names—Moni, Mary—sounded like Minnie's, and that may have made Minnie feel close to them, too.

Two: The Ants' Wedding

In 1898, when Minnie was almost seven years old, North Carolina's black members of Congress were voted out of office. A white mob gathered in Wilmington to gloat over the victory. The whites burned a building that housed a black newspaper and shot at least twelve innocent black bystanders. "For the first time in my life I have been ashamed of my state," wrote a white woman who lived in Wilmington. "There was not a shadow of an excuse for what occurred."

Afraid of more violence, hundreds of black citizens abandoned their homes and businesses. They hid in cold swamps outside the city and waited for the white race riot to end.

No one in the family remembers if Minnie and her family were among those who fled. But Rachel left Wilmington early in 1899, "just as soon as it closed [when the trouble ended]," and moved to New York. She married for the third time, and died five years later. Minnie never saw her great-grandmother again.

The racism that caused the riot lingered like a sour note throughout the state for years. In 1901 a law was passed forcing blacks to sit in the back of streetcars, and in 1904 saloons were segregated. Five black North Carolinians were lynched between 1900 and 1905.

During this anxious time, Mary sent Minnie to live for a year with Mary's sister, Aunt Hagar, in Norfolk, Virginia. While in Norfolk, Minnie attended a two-room school. One day the principal caught her drawing. He cruelly struck her hand "hard" with a piece of bamboo fishing pole. "You can't draw and get your lessons," he lectured her. None of Minnie's childhood drawings survive, and their subjects are not known. Perhaps by that time, she felt the need to draw some of her many dreams.

After Minnie returned to Wilmington, disturbing dreams continued to leave her exhausted. Her fatigue made school difficult. "I had to repeat my fourth grade because I didn't do well," Minnie admitted later. "I didn't get my arithmetic." She en-

Untitled [interior scene with dragon]. This royal couple could be Paris, the Trojan prince, and Helen, the kidnaped Greek queen. 9 x 11¾. Courtesy of Luise Ross Gallery, New York, and the Minnie Evans Estate.

joyed history, though, especially stories about the Greeks and the Trojans. "That's all I studied, all I loved," she remembered. "I love to read about the gods."

One teacher, Rebecca Lawson, remembered Minnie as a "perfect lady." Another, Mrs. Alice Jackson, loved to hear eleven-year-old Minnie read aloud. But some-

times Mrs. Jackson thought she was avoiding schoolwork. One day she asked Minnie about her droopy eyes. "Minnie, what on earth!" she said. "What's the matter with you?"

"I'm just tired and sleepy," Minnie complained. "I don't rest . . . I don't sleep at night." She felt so weary from dream-

Untitled [head with angels and winged horse]. Minnie's love of mythology may have inspired this griffinlike creature.
11 x 13¾. Collection of Robert Fargo Art Gallery, Tuscaloosa, Ala. Courtesy of Luise Ross Gallery, New York, and the Minnie Evans Estate.

ing that she was almost relieved when she had to quit school after finishing the fifth grade. Money was scarce, and there wasn't enough to buy school clothes. "I was willing to work," she said later. "I wanted a little money."

Sometime after 1905, Mama Mary, Ella, and Minnie moved from Wilmington to nearby Wrightsville Beach. There Ella met a man named Joe Kelly, who had two grown daughters. Ella married Joe in 1908. Finally Minnie had a father, a sweet and "merry" man whom she could call Papa.

Minnie joined Ella and Papa Joe's two

Untitled [atomic bomb]. Shortly before her wedding, Minnie dreamed of airplanes that she called "mosquito hawks." 11¾ x 9. Courtesy of Luise Ross Gallery, New York, and the Minnie Evans Estate.

daughters as a gatherer. Together they picked oysters from the sound and carried the heavy buckets to the city, where they sold the shellfish for ten cents a quart. Minnie earned two dollars and fifty cents a week for her labor and later said that she "loved it."

Although Minnie's formal education stopped at the end of fifth grade, she continued to learn from the natural world. As a gatherer, she spent most of her time near the shore. Every morning she watched the sun climb out of the Atlantic Ocean to the east. When she faced west at dusk, she saw the sun slip silently into the waters of the sound.

Minnie never forgot the beauty of the sunrise and sunset. Years later, the image of sun over water appeared often in her art, as shown in the rising and setting sun of *Untitled [head with angels and winged horse].*

In 1908, Papa Joe's daughters introduced fifteen-year-old Minnie to Julius Caesar Evans, a southern gentleman with quiet ways. Julius worked on the lavish Pembroke Park estate in Wrightsville Beach.

Pembroke Jones, a wealthy native of Wilmington, had purchased the three-thousand-acre estate in the late 1880s and named it after himself. Then he hired his son-in-law, John Russell Pope, who was a well-known architect, to design the gardens and a hunting lodge.

Julius was one of the twenty coachmen who worked for Pembroke Jones. Wearing a top hat and tails, Julius drove Jones's family and friends over the twenty-eight miles of oyster-shell roads that twisted through the park.

Untitled [winged animal, devil with snakes, face]. The angels and devil reveal Minnie's definite ideas about heaven and hell. 11 x 13¾. Collection of the Akron Art Museum, Museum Acquisition Fund in Memory of Honorary Trustee, Jean Palmer Wade. Courtesy of Luise Ross Gallery, New York, and the Minnie Evans Estate.

Minnie knew that nineteen-year-old Julius was "stuck" on her. He escorted her to church "a time or two," then asked her to marry him. Minnie was too young to be legally married and asked Joe's daughters for advice. "Marry Julius if he wants you," the young women said. Minnie decided that getting married "would be fun." She agreed to become Julius's wife in December 1908, four days after her sixteenth birthday. They were wed in the green five-room tenant house where

Julius lived on the Pembroke Park estate.

Minnie recorded her age as eighteen on the marriage certificate. A gentle jester with a playful wit, she chuckled about this deceit for the rest of her life. Julius was a "lovely" man, she recalled, and they had three sons, all born in the tenant house between 1910 and 1915. Pembroke Jones named Minnie's children after three of his hunting buddies, Elisha, David, and George. All were millionaires who made their fortunes on Wall Street, the financial district of New York City.

"I had four boys," Minnie joked years later. "I call them my four because I had to take care of [Julius] like a boy."

For the first eight years of her marriage, Minnie was a housewife. As she matured from a young girl into a wife and mother, the strong side of her personality began to appear. When she was a child she had learned the difference between right and wrong at home, in school, and at church. Now she turned these lessons into strict rules for her boys.

George Evans, Minnie's son, recalled that he and his brothers often fought with each other. Minnie whipped their legs with switches that left scars—a common form of punishment used by some parents in those days. Although she could be

Untitled [devils, angels under starry sky]. Like the trickster devil in African-American folklore, this group of rascals looks more playful than evil. 12 x 9. Courtesy of New Jersey State Museum.

humorous and loving, especially with youngsters, Minnie had a stern side to her nature, too.

Like many African-Americans, Minnie found strength in what she called the "daily food" of her religious faith. St. Matthew's African Methodist Episcopal Church was only a few miles away from Pembroke Park. Every Sunday while the boys were growing up, the Evans family attended Sunday school, a church service, or a Bible study group called the Christian/Devil League.

As Minnie grew older, her religious beliefs became more rigid. Sometimes she and Julius argued when he thought she prayed too much, and they disagreed over her interest in the teachings of the Jehovah's Witnesses. Minnie never raised her voice during these quarrels, but she refused to hear other opinions. "This is the way it is," Minnie would announce, "and that's that!"

Minnie may have needed to control others because she could not control the visions that filled her mind. Being married seemed to stop some of the worst dreams. She no longer thought prophets carried her to the "boneyard" at night. But she continued to see odd images during the day. "I had day visions," she said in an interview. "They would take advantage of me."

One evening as she walked home from work, she looked through a hole in a hollow rotten log. Minnie thought she saw lights twinkling inside, and suddenly she thought she was in the log with some ants. They were at a wedding with a "beautiful bride," flower girls, and a minister. They spoke a strange language as they stared at her. "Was I an ant?" she wondered later. "Or did I look like some kind of a little awkward insect to them?"

Minnie told Julius about the vision, but he thought it was one of the "silliest" stories he had ever heard. "Minnie, don't ever tell that to anybody else," he said. "They'll think you're crazy."

"Crazy." To Minnie, the word must have seemed like her middle name. She had a fine husband whom she loved. She had three sons who were always respectful to her. But her dreams and visions made her feel confused and alone. "So many [people]," she said later, "do not understand."

Three: The Plantation

Whn Minnie's youngest son, George, was three years old, she began her long employment on the Pembroke Park estate. Julius still worked at Pembroke Park, and he may have helped her find a job there. In 1916 she began working as a maid in the elegant estate mansion.

The Victorian structure was originally built as a hotel, with wide porches, many living rooms and bedrooms, and a large ballroom. One of a hundred employees on the estate, Minnie helped keep the rambling house clean.

Both black and white people in Wilmington refer to Pembroke Park as "the plantation." Before the Civil War, that term meant any farm with more than twenty slaves working it. Jones bought the estate twenty years after the Civil War and slavery ended, but in some ways he treated his employees like slaves.

Plantation owners often named their slaves' children, as Pembroke Jones had named Minnie's boys. And they usually let the slaves have extra food at Christmas-time. In the same way, Pembroke Jones and his wife, Sadie, let Minnie ask friends to a yearly Christmas party. Held somewhere on the estate, Minnie's holiday affair featured fancy food that may have been left over from the Joneses' annual children's Christmas party.

There were some advantages to working for the Joneses. Minnie Evans's granddaughter Minnie Clauson recalled that her grandmother enjoyed seeing the powerful people who visited Pembroke Park. She also enjoyed the lavish display of wealth.

Jones once held a moonlit party for fifty people in a tree house that was built especially for the event. Guests arrived in a horse-drawn carriage driven by Julius Evans, then climbed a staircase that circled a huge live oak. When the diners reached the platform at the top, they found tables covered with snowy linen and set with fine silver. For party favors, each guest received a piece of diamond jewelry or a watch.

Working for Pembroke Jones allowed

Minnie to feel connected to the gilded world of the rich. It also gave the Evans family another small but steady income. Despite the benefits, though, the Wilmington area was similar to other southern towns.

Black and white neighborhoods were next to each other, but segregated by race. If Minnie had to stand on a crowded streetcar or bus, she stood next to black and white passengers alike. When seats were available, though, she had to sit in the back. "White in front, Colored in rear" read the sign on every Wilmington bus.

With no black policemen, firemen, or government officials in Wilmington or Wrightsville Beach, African-Americans learned to survive by keeping silent. Members of Minnie's generation were especially reserved. As children and grandchildren of former slaves, they were taught to cooperate in public and laugh in private, where "Mr. Charlie" (any white man) couldn't hear.

Once a white friend asked Minnie about the race riot of 1898. Minnie had little to say. She replied only that "they [white people] just gets that way sometimes."

Yet there is no doubt that racism affect-ed Minnie and her family. Her son George worked for Mrs. Pembroke Jones when he was a child. George lived in a room in the estate mansion. As footman for Mrs. Jones's carriage, he held the reins to the horse and carried her pocketbook.

When Sadie Jones needed him, she rang a bell. If he didn't arrive quickly enough, she hit his legs with a riding crop. "She had her ways," George recalled.

Few people ever heard Minnie complain about her white employers. Nor do we know how she felt when white folks in the area used the too familiar "Aunt Minnie" instead of the more respectful "Miss Minnie."

She never talked openly about these slights, even though discrimination touched her life every day. After years of being called crazy, she had learned to keep hurt feelings inside.

Four: The Angel That Stands by Me

In 1919, Pembroke Jones died. Three years later his widow, Sadie Jones, married the wealthy financier Henry Walters. They moved to Airlie, a nearby estate that Sadie inherited from Jones. Minnie and Julius stayed in the tenant house in Pembroke Park, but continued working as maid and caretaker for Mrs. Walters at Airlie.

After Henry Walters died in 1931, Mrs. Walters decided to turn the one-hundred-and-fifty-five-acre Airlie estate into Airlie Gardens. Over the next twelve years, employees planted more than a million azalea bushes and thousands of camellia bushes. George Evans remembered working as a handyman in the gardens, watering azaleas from the many spigots along Airlie's winding roads.

Minnie's dreaming continued through these years. Then on Thanksgiving Day, 1935, Mama Mary died in Minnie's living room. After that, every Thanksgiving reminded Minnie of her "pal," the woman who had said Minnie would do something

Lakeside, Airlie Gardens, Wilmington, North Carolina. Courtesy of the author.

wonderful in life. Earlier that year, Minnie *had* done something wonderful. The event seemed so ordinary, though, that no one, not even Minnie, realized what had happened.

Two days before Easter Sunday, 1935, she began drawing on a scrap of paper bag she had used for a grocery list. Although she didn't understand the "funny things" she drew, she made another picture the next day. Minnie sketched a few more pictures, then slipped them between the pages of a *Redbook* magazine and forgot about them.

When she burned a stack of old magazines in the late 1930s, her drawings, later named *"My Very First"* and *"My Second,"* fell to the ground. Since fate had rescued these pictures from the fire, she decided that they must be special.

Beginning on that day, Minnie Evans took herself seriously as an artist. Drawing freehand from left to right, she first sketched an outline in pencil. Then she applied rainbow colors with crayons. Later she also used watercolors and oil paints.

Working on discarded paper, she created up to seven pictures a day. Later she said she felt as if an "engine" drove her hand. According to Minnie, no one taught her how to draw or paint. "God has sent me teachers," she said. "The angel that stands by me, answers me . . . and directs me what to do."

Minnie's mother, Ella, lived with Papa Joe just a few blocks away. She begged her only child to stop drawing and painting. "Minnie, it's affecting your mind," she declared.

Minnie's obsession was puzzling to Ella. The country was still suffering from a financial depression in the late 1930s. These were hard years, especially in the South, and most people saved their energy for work.

"My Very First" and *"My Second."* At the bottom of *"My Second,"* strange animals seem to be swimming around a boat filled with people. 5½ x 7⅞ and 5¾ x 7⅝. Courtesy of Whitney Museum of American Art.

Minnie's husband, Julius, didn't understand her need to create art either. "Minnie, why?" he asked his wife. In Minnie's day, women cooked, cleaned, and sewed, but Minnie often forgot to fix breakfast or sweep the floor. When she returned home from Airlie at the end of the day, she didn't feel like doing household chores again. All she wanted to do was draw.

Sometimes Minnie sketched an entire picture, erased it, then spent days drawing the same image again. "I keep putting down something till after a while something says, 'That's right, Minnie, that's right. All right.'"

Most of her pictures are filled with multiple eyes. "I don't know where so many of them come from," she said. If she tried to "outen," or erase, them, she was compelled to put them in again. She felt that even the choice of color was beyond her control — if she decided to use a green tube of paint, her hand would move to the blue. "I can't ask myself any questions about this whatever," Minnie said of her colors. "So I just do . . . what it comes to me to do."

Seldom without a pencil or brush in her hand at home, she sometimes drew or

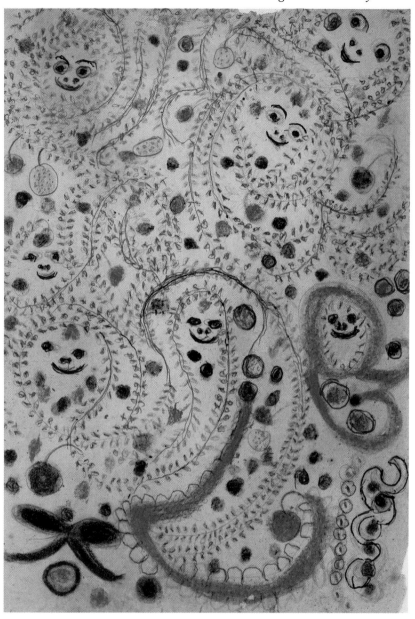

Untitled [trailing green vine with face]. Most of Minnie's early drawings were designs of dots, circles, triangles, and half-moon faces. 7¼ x 5. Collection of Barbara Smith. Courtesy of Luise Ross Gallery, New York, and the Minnie Evans Estate.

Untitled [head with green leaves, red flowers, butterflies]. One of Minnie's many paintings with multiple eyes. 16 x 20.
Collection of Michael Coffindaffer. Courtesy of Luise Ross Gallery, New York, and the Minnie Evans Estate.

painted through the day, forgetting to eat or drink. Often she got up in the middle of the night to paint a dream.

Minnie seemed so driven that the Evans family feared she was going insane. They worried she would have to go to an asylum. In a fit of frustration, Julius took the drawings away from her. When Min-nie couldn't make pictures, though, she got sick.

The images in her mind haunted her. "Those things got on me," she said. "No one knows. If I didn't paint, seem like I would die." She later recalled that she was in "very, very bad shape."

One day in 1944, a storm seemed to

spin inside Minnie's head, and she lost track of time. Years later, Minnie's mother would say, "The sun was way over there and she hadn't washed a dish, hadn't swept the floor, hadn't made up her bed."

Minnie paced the floor all day, praying for God to deliver her from the "terrible feeling" that burdened her. Late that afternoon, she walked into the back yard. Crows flew out of the woods, covered the roof of her house, and filled the branches of nearby trees. To Minnie, the crows were a sign from God.

"I got no one here to hear me," Minnie said. "God has sent the ravens out of the woods just to hear me pray." She was convinced that God had revealed his presence to her.

Although she had joined the church as a child, now the Lord had called her as an adult. She would share her experience with others by letting her pictures talk for her. Asking for a "clean heart" and the "right spirit," she prayed not to get too "biggety" about her gift.

Minnie resumed her art with a passion. Julius became desperate and went to his pastor for help. "My Minnie's gone crazy," Julius told him. The pastor understood Minnie's great need to create pictures and asked Julius and Ella to let her

alone. George Rountree, Jr., a Wilmington lawyer and Minnie's lifelong friend, advised her to use her talent, to "go ahead and paint."

"I did that," Minnie remembered, "and that was wonderful."

Five: God Dressed This World in Green

In 1944, the fifty-two-year-old artist began drawing and painting on larger, nine-by-twelve-inch discarded Coast Guard stationery. Her images changed too. As her style evolved, she began to mix designs with what she called "reallyistic" scenes. She created more detailed faces and mouths, and her simple leaves became more complicated.

By then, Airlie had become one of the showcase gardens of the South. It also became an important element in the art of Minnie Evans. Mrs. Walters had died in 1943, and Airlie was bought by Albert Corbett in 1947. He moved his wife and sons into the mansion. After forty years of

saving, Minnie and Julius could afford to have a home built. They left the tenant house in Pembroke Park and moved into a new white frame house nearby.

The following year Corbett hired Minnie to collect admission fees from visitors to the grounds. At first there was no gatehouse, so she sat in the leafy shade of an oak tree that sheltered her in hot weather. About three years later, Corbett had a dark green wooden gatehouse built.

For the next twenty-four years—March through September, seven days a week, from nine in the morning until dusk—Minnie Evans sat in the cramped booth and collected admission fees from thousands of visitors.

She earned ten dollars a week, or about sixteen cents an hour. Because there was no bathroom near the gatehouse, Minnie brought a pickle jar to use behind the

Statue of Greek god Pan at Airlie Gardens. Statues of mythological figures kept Minnie company during quiet off-season months at Airlie Gardens.
Courtesy of the author.

Untitled [women with tears and writing]. Minnie signed some paintings with her initials.
9½ x 7. Courtesy of Luise Ross Gallery, New York, and the Minnie Evans Estate.

"Design: Airlie Garden." Unlike most of Minnie's abstract designs, this one is asymmetrical. 16 x 20. Collection American Shaker, Courtesy of Luise Ross Gallery, New York.

building. Often lonely, she was discouraged by her employers from talking to friends who visited her.

Still, Minnie found a calming peace in the cool green gardens. To her the outdoors was a church whose architect was God. During breaks between visitors, she dozed, dreaming of the beauty she found in the natural world. *"Design: Airlie Garden,"* a vivid painting of one of these dreams, is alive with blooming flowers, lush plants, and butterflies.

Minnie gave her art to anyone who seemed interested. Always attentive to youngsters, she gave pictures to Albert Corbett's grandchildren, who had no use for them and threw them away.

But many of Airlie's visitors admired Minnie's works. Like other self-taught artists, she was surprised when people offered to buy her drawings and paintings. Encouraged by their interest, she hung completed pictures from the white wrought-iron gates near the gatehouse. These she sold for fifty cents each, or the equivalent of more than a half day's salary. Soon word spread about Minnie, and people came just to see the artist at Airlie.

The artist, like her art, left a strong impression on everyone she met. Some people saw only the serious side of her nature. One early collector recalls that she was a "heavy-set" woman who quietly watched him look through her pictures. A former museum director recollects that she was a "grumpy old woman" who "sulked" when he wouldn't buy a drawing.

Loss of family members, aging, and ill health might have made Minnie cranky. In 1954, her "jolly" Papa Joe died, and Ella moved in with Julius and Minnie. Then Julius died of diabetes in 1956. In her sixties and growing deaf, Minnie had diabetes too.

Yet others remember Minnie as a charming woman of good humor and dignity. A Wilmington artist recalls that she greeted him with jokes as she tried to coax him into buying a painting. A "perfect lady," she spoke in a courtly fashion with a sweet southern voice.

After Minnie's reputation grew, the Artists' Gallery in Wilmington (now the St. John's Museum) held an exhibit of her work in 1961. The following year, she met someone who would tell the rest of the world about the visionary art of Minnie Evans.

Six: Beautiful Dreamer

When Nina Howell Starr first saw Minnie's pictures in late 1961, they hurt her eyes. "I wasn't mad about them," Nina said. "They blinded me—the colors, you know." At fifty-eight, Nina was completing a master's degree in fine-art photography at the University of Florida. Like Minnie, she was beginning a career as an artist. She had already exhibited her photographs in three solo shows. She had also published two articles on folk artists like Minnie—people who create art without formal training.

When a friend of Nina's spied Minnie's crayon drawings hanging on the Airlie gate, she bought five for Nina to see. Nina had to return the pictures to her friend, but first she photographed them so she could study them more carefully. She took black-and-white photographs of Minnie's work, then developed the film in her own darkroom.

"I was printing those pictures, and that's when I was so startled," Nina recalled. With the "color bleached out," she noticed the design and balance of Minnie's drawings.

A detail from Minnie's drawing of two veiled women is shown opposite. This picture was especially "moving and creative" to Nina. "That's the one," Nina said in an interview, "that turned my life."

The photographer had seen the art. Now she was ready to meet the artist. Early in 1962, she drove her wood-sided Ford station wagon from Florida to Minnie's home in Wrightsville Beach. There Nina tape-recorded the first of many interviews she made with Minnie between 1962 and 1973.

Minnie expressed her strong religious beliefs in this first interview. "I do not like card playing!" she preached into the tape recorder. "I have always thought it's a sin!" Before Nina left that day, Minnie asked her small grandson to sing the hymn "Jesus Loves Me" into the machine.

By the end of Nina and Minnie's first day together, there was a mutual respect between the two women. "Thank you,

Untitled [detail of veiled women]. Minnie Evans frequently drew scallop, spiral, and leaf designs.
Courtesy of Nina Howell Starr.

madam," Minnie declared when Nina left that first afternoon. "You have added to my life today." The next day she announced, "Mrs. Starr's going to put some life in me!"

Despite differences in race and education, the two women had much in common. Unlike many women of their generation who stayed at home and took care of grandchildren, Nina and Minnie had become artists. Also, each had a confident, often prickly, manner.

Once a museum left Nina out of an exhibit. "I had some very good photographs of women," she wrote in an article, "and should have been included in the show."

Minnie, too, was strong-willed. There were quarrels after George and his wife, children, and grandchildren moved into Minnie's house. According to her granddaughter, Minnie Clauson, Minnie "ruled" the family, especially George, and she usually got her own way.

When the interview was over, Nina wanted to borrow some of Minnie's works so she could photograph them in her motel room, but Minnie was reluctant to part with them. During the interview, Minnie had mentioned George Rountree, Jr., her "best friend." The next day, Nina found the lawyer's name in the phone book, met him in his office, and explained her problem.

Rountree rode with Nina in her car to Airlie Gardens and convinced Minnie that she could trust Nina with her art.

Nina Starr became a great comfort to Minnie. When Nina met her, the Evans family lived in what her son George called a "thick," or crowded, neighborhood. Folks often stopped to chat while she sat painting at an easel on her porch. Yet she remembered that even as she worked they "cut their eyes away" and ignored her art.

"My people," Minnie said, "became jealous because the white people would praise me." Her granddaughter suggests that Minnie might have offended the neighbors because she felt superior to them.

Nina, however, took a great interest in Minnie's pictures. Over the next two decades, Nina sold Minnie's art without commission, while pursuing her own photography. "I rode the two careers in tandem," Nina recalled. Handling her career and Minnie's at the same time was not always easy, though. Sometimes, she said, "It was almost a conflict."

With Nina's help, Minnie's career grew slowly but steadily during the 1960s. Nina stored more than five hundred drawings at a time in her home in New York City. She promoted sales of Minnie's art by writing articles and talking to art dealers and often traveled to Wilmington at her own expense.

In 1966 Nina arranged Minnie's first New York exhibit. The Church of the Epiphany showed Minnie's pictures twice in April 1966, and St. Clement's Episcopal Church displayed them in May 1966. Minnie called Nina the "president of my pictures in New York."

Nina's knowledge of the art world helped her guide Minnie's career. She asked her to sign and date older works and all new art. Minnie agreed, though she had trouble estimating dates for pictures she had completed ten or twenty years earlier. As a result, many dates are incorrect. Not all of the signatures are Minnie's, either — in the early 1960s, Minnie asked her granddaughter to sign her pictures for her.

Most of Minnie Evans's works are untitled, with titles assigned by someone else.

"Lost Indian." Minnie said that the light in the sky was a signal to help the lost Indian find his way. 9⅝ x 7¹⁄₁₆. Courtesy of Richard Edson and the Folk Art Gallery, Baltimore, Maryland.

Occasionally, she wrote a title on the back of a picture like *"Lost Indian"* and *"Design:*

Airlie Garden." Nina Starr modified at least one title when she changed *"Funny Green Animal"* to *"Green Animal."* "The words were not dignified," Nina said in an interview in 1994. "I wanted to bury them."

Maybe she sensed that the informal style of Minnie's rural black English might not appeal to art collectors from the North. Nina knew Minnie needed money and believed changing titles was "necessary" at the beginning of her friend's career.

Minnie's need for funds was "very real and very important," recalled Nina. Sometimes Minnie wrote to borrow money from her. "I am in distress so I am asking you to lend me fifty dollars," she wrote in 1965. But Minnie repaid her debts as soon as she could. "I'm not a bum," she explained in the letter.

In the late 1960s a Minnie Evans painting sold for thirty-five to seventy-five dollars. When someone bought a picture, all of the money went directly into Minnie's bank account. She didn't become an artist for profit, but she welcomed the extra income.

Like many folk artists, Minnie never supported herself with income from her art. During her lifetime, the most money she earned for one work was eight hun-

"Green Animal." Minnie Evans made a series of paintings of this animal, sometimes calling it the *"Green Unicorn."* 8¾ x 11½. Courtesy of Nina Howell Starr.

dred dollars. Depending on the size, they sell now for one thousand to fifteen thousand dollars.

In August 1969, the Art Image Gallery in New York featured an exhibition of Minnie's work. Then an article about the show appeared in *Newsweek*. The writer of the article called Minnie a "beautiful dreamer" who was "breathtakingly gifted." Nina Starr was thrilled for her friend. Nina wrote to *Newsweek* and thanked the editor for sharing "the wonder" of Minnie Evans's life and work with the rest of the country.

Seven: His Eye Is on the Sparrow

Minnie's success as an artist did not lessen her interest in St. Matthew's African Methodist Episcopal Church. She kept her membership in the choir and enjoyed singing the words to her beloved hymn: "His eye is on the sparrow—and I know He's watching me!"

After Julius died, Minnie continued her visits to "speaking meetings" at nearby black churches, including Pilgrim's Rest Baptist Church. "Now we will hear from Minnie Evans," the minister would announce.

Minnie's eyes flashed and her forefinger pointed toward heaven as she spoke in a commanding voice. "We will *be* like the angels in heaven!" she liked to say.

Her testimonials were not unusual. Black women have had a long history of ministry in both Africa and America. In some West African religions, black women are spirit mediums who believe they can talk with the spirits of gods and ancestors. Rhythmic dancing, singing, and clapping help a medium go into a trance. As one African has described it, the

St. Matthew's African Methodist Episcopal Church, Wilmington, North Carolina. Courtesy of the author.

women "speak with the mouth of a spirit."

Once in the New World, enslaved Africans had to abandon African religious practices and adapt to the religion of the slaveholder. In the South, many became Baptists. In Wilmington, they often chose the African Methodist Episcopal Church, as Minnie did after she grew up.

Baptist and Methodist revivals were especially appealing to southern African-Americans. At revivals, people spoke to God through singing, clapping, and shouting—rituals that recalled the ecstatic trances of West Africa. American black

"Speak, Lord." Nina Howell Starr said this photograph of Minnie demonstrated the "enduring power" of women. Courtesy of Nina Howell Starr and Photo-Researchers, New York City.

women like Minnie were as active in this experience as their foremothers had been in Africa.

Some of Minnie's art serves as a bridge between the religious traditions of the two continents. The open book in *"Modern Art"* looks like a Bible, a symbol of Minnie's Christian faith. But the mystical writing on its pages recalls her racial heritage, too. Several art historians think that the symbols look African.

What was the meaning of the mysterious symbols that Minnie painted? Perhaps they were her way of paying respect to the words in the Bible. Or maybe they were her symbols for the written word.

Her own Mama Mary and great-grand-mother Rachel had been forbidden as slaves to learn to read and write; Ella could not read either. So the symbols might have been Minnie's way of showing the importance of literacy. But even the artist was unable to explain her art. "When I get through with them I have to look at them like somebody else," she said of her drawings. "They are just as strange to me as they are to anybody else."

During the 1960s, Minnie added angels like those in *"A Dream"* (November 1968) to her collection of painted creatures. Nina once asked Minnie why she painted white angels. "I paint imitations of angels

"Modern Art." Rainbows appear often in Minnie's art. A fortuneteller once told her that she was "standing in a rainbow." 14½ x 20. Courtesy of Luise Ross Gallery, New York, and the Minnie Evans Estate.

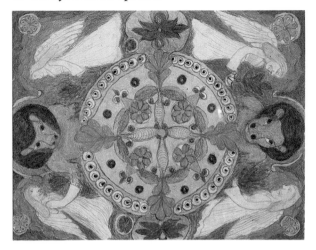

"A Dream." Some art historians think the oriental rugs and artwork at Pembroke Park estate influenced Minnie's art. But she said, *"My drawings do not come from . . . Mrs. [Pembroke Jones's] homes. They come from my head. Still coming."* 16 x 20. Courtesy of Luise Ross Gallery, New York, and the Minnie Evans Estate.

Minnie also drew hundreds of elaborate faces in the 1960s. Art critics have noticed their Far Eastern quality. Minnie said she didn't dream about black people, yet she often dreamed of "Chinamans." And when she dreamed of "everything in yellow," she wondered if that was a "sign of something in China." Like most artists, Minnie was intrigued by physical features that were different from her own.

Untitled [head, butterflies with staring eyes]. A universal image of all humankind, this face could belong to any man, woman, color, or nation. 11¾ x 9. Collection of Robert and Deborah Cummins. Courtesy of Luise Ross Gallery, New York, and the Minnie Evans Estate.

just as I've imagined them." Minnie explained. "I do not believe there is an artist born who can paint an angel, because they come from the throne of God." Skin color was not a issue for Minnie — only accuracy.

Perhaps she imagined only white angels because she did not see a picture of a black one until she was almost eighty years old. Before the late 1960s, illustrated editions of the Bible portrayed Jesus and other biblical figures with white skin. Angels in Christmas Nativity scenes were always white. Even the faces in the stained-glass windows of black churches were made from milky white glass.

Eight: This Is My Heart

Although Minnie said she had "thousands and thousands left to draw" and more strange visions in her life than she "had ever told of," her pace slowed during the 1970s. In 1974, she retired from Airlie Gardens at the age of eighty-two. By this time, she was a celebrated American folk artist.

Links, a national organization of African-American women, had honored her at a luncheon in Wilmington in 1969. The National Museum of American Art in Washington, D.C., accepted her gift of *"Design Made at Airlie Garden"* in 1975, and Jo Kallenborn, one of Minnie's friends in Wilmington, held a celebration luncheon for her.

That same year, the Whitney Museum of Art in New York displayed Minnie's pictures. Nina Starr organized the exhibit. Titled "Minnie Evans," it was shown for several hot weeks in July and August of 1975. Neither the Jones nor the Corbett families, who had employed Minnie for more than fifty years, attended these events

or congratulated her on her success. If Minnie knew of their snubs, she probably didn't care. "Mama [Minnie] had high self-esteem," recalled her granddaughter. "She could have sat with the queen of England."

The art world often calls self-taught artists like Minnie "outsiders." Artists with formal training are familiar with art books and magazines, dealers, critics, and museums. But self-taught artists are usually unaware of this professional world.

Not everyone likes outsider art. One artist from the South has called it "anti-art." If outsiders are in the museums, he fretted in an interview, where will we show the "real" art? A museum official said that Minnie's art was what he would expect of someone who sat all day in a gatehouse.

Yet there are many collectors who admire the bold colors of outsider art. They also like the art because it tells the story of the artist's life. Others are drawn to the power of the artist's personality. As Jo Kallenborn pointed out, some people

"Design Made at Airlie Garden." Every inch of the canvas delivers a colorful sermon on the harmony of nature. 19¾ x 23¾. Courtesy of the National Museum of American Art.

Still, Minnie's outward enjoyment of fame seemed unrelated to the inner world of the artist. When she heard that a London gallery was showing some of her pictures, she had no desire to attend the exhibit. "I ain't going that far," she said, "to see something I done did." Her son George once asked her how it felt to be famous. Minnie replied with a laugh, "I don't know. I can't feel it! I can't realize it, you know."

In the late 1970s, George and his family moved into their own home. Minnie and her mother lived by themselves for a few years in Minnie's white house. After they became too frail to be alone, they moved in with George and some of his children and grandchildren.

Her health failing, Minnie continued to paint while living with five generations under one roof, although she admitted that her hand was "not as steady now" as it used to be.

By 1980, walking was quite painful for Minnie. Jo Kallenborn recalled that diabetes made Minnie's feet look like "gnarled

loved Minnie so much that they worked for her free of charge, including Minnie's lawyer, George Rountree, Jr., and Nina Howell Starr.

Perhaps because Minnie felt slighted by the black community, attention from the black press was important to her. Jo Kallenborn recalled that Minnie complained when Nina wrote an article about her in the feminist magazine *Ms.* "I don't want nothing to do with that old magazine," Minnie fussed. "I don't know why I can't make *Ebony!*"

Untitled [self-portrait]. The serenity of Minnie's self-portrait resembles that found in her painting of female faces on page 12. 17 x 12. Collection of George Evans. Photograph courtesy of Wellington B. Gray Gallery, East Carolina University, Greenville, North Carolina.

sweet potatoes," and Minnie complained about her "weak knees." Yet she was able to attend an exhibit of her art at St. John's Museum in October 1980. From her wheelchair she looked around at the dreams she had brought to life, and sighed, "This is my heart."

In 1981 Minnie's mother died at the age of one hundred and two. The next year the ninety-year-old Minnie entered a nursing home. It was there that she first viewed the movie made about her. Although her memory was failing, she mouthed every word that she had spoken in the film. Still driven by her dreams, she continued to paint pictures in the nursing home. The quality of these final paintings is understandably poor.

Minnie Evans died of kidney failure in 1987, four days after her ninety-fifth birthday. "I love people to a certain extent," she once said, "but sometimes I want to get off in the garden to talk with God."

For Minnie, the end of life in this world was a pathway to the next. "We won't know each other in heaven," she declared. "I don't care if I know anybody or not," she said with a joyous laugh. "I just want to be in there!"

Many frustrating years had to pass before Minnie's family understood her need

Minnie Evans's grave, Wilmington, North Carolina.
Courtesy of the author.

to create art. She once said that Julius accepted her gift only after she "got to the gate" and people bought her pictures. Her son Elisha admitted that his mother knew what she was doing all along, even though the family didn't realize her talent.

People called Minnie crazy, and she often felt set apart from others. Yet she used her special view of the world to complete the spiritual task she felt that God had given her. With her art, she passed on the message she found in her dreams and visions—the religious faith that she called her "guarantee" of love.

Afterword

May 14, 1994, was an important date for Greenville, North Carolina: The mayor proclaimed it "Minnie Evans Day." With that announcement, a meeting, art exhibit, family reunion, barbecue, and gospel sing began. Northerners came south, white people swayed to black gospel music, and men and women wept. For three days, a community of family, friends, art collectors, and scholars celebrated the memory of Minnie Evans.

The weekend began with an exhibit of 130 of her works. This was the latest in a series of twenty solo exhibitions and fifty-nine group shows. A discussion of her place in the art world followed the exhibit. Everyone had different interpretations of her pictures. Still, all agreed that whether she was called a folk artist, an outsider artist, a self-taught artist, a visionary artist, or simply an American artist, Minnie Evans had made a special contribution to the world of art.

Just as a dream can be hard to describe in words, Minnie's art can be difficult to explain. Some art critics call her work childlike and primitive, but others compare it to modern art by trained artists. Many collectors are riveted by her pictures, but a few are troubled by the eyes that stare from most of her works. Minnie's son George remembers that one man returned a picture because he said the eyes kept him awake at night.

Those who knew Minnie are convinced that she was different from everyone else: Her lawyer, George Rountree, Jr., once commented that she would always be a "mystery" to him. In the 1983 film, Nina Howell Starr said, "I really feel that Minnie has powers that not many of us have." But her granddaughter stated it best. "Minnie Evans," she said, was an artist who was "out of her time."

Finally, though, it is the art that matters. Like the dreams that inspired them, each of her works is a tapestry floating in a timeless space. And just behind that curtain of mysterious detail, an enchanted Eden waits to reveal itself: the visionary paradise of Minnie Evans.

Notes

Chapter 1: *A Very Peculiar Life*

Minnie Evans told the story about elephants in a documentary by Irving Saraf and Allie Light, *The Angel That Stands by Me: Minnie Evans's Art* (San Francisco: Light-Saraf Folk Arts, 1983. Distributed by The Stutz Co., Berkeley, Calif.).

The story about the prophets is from a typescript of interviews with Minnie conducted by Nina Howell Starr, Wilmington, N.C., 1969–1973. The typescript, "Conversations with Minnie Evans," is among the personal papers of Nina Howell Starr. A copy is in the library of the North Carolina Museum of Art, Raleigh, N.C.

Nathan Comfort Starr, Nina's husband, compared Minnie to William Blake in "The Unique Folk Artist of Airlie," *The State* (Raleigh, N.C.), March 1, 1969, pp. 16–17.

Biographical information about Minnie Evans's ancestors was gathered from Nina Starr's typescript; Starr's personal notes from visits with Minnie Evans; and the author's interview with George Evans, May 16, 1993, Wilmington, N.C.

Chapter 2: *The Ants' Wedding*

Details about the Wilmington race riot are from *The Promise of the New South: Life After Reconstruction* by Edward L. Ayers (New York: Oxford University Press, 1992), p. 302; *The Quest for Progress: The Way We Lived in North Carolina 1870–1920* by Sidney Nathans (Chapel Hill, N.C.: University of North Carolina Press, 1993), pp. 81–83; "The Clansman on Stage and Screen" by John C. Inscoe, *North Carolina Historical Review*, April 1987, pp. 139–161.

George Evans described church services at St. Matthew's African Methodist Episcopal Church in an interview with the author on May 16, 1993. Remarks by Minnie Evans about her sons are from *The Angel That Stands by Me*.

Chapter 3: *The Plantation*

Information about Pembroke Park was taken from a telephone interview with the director of the St. John's Museum in Wilmington, C. Reynolds Brown, on September 2, 1994; *Wilmington's Vanished Homes and Buildings* by Emma Woodward Macmillan (Raleigh, N.C.: Edwards and Broughton Co., 1966), p. 85; and "Landfall: The Way It Was," an address by Barbara Hopper to the Great Oak Club (Wilmington, N.C.: November 10, 1993).

Minnie Clauson recalled riding a crowded bus with her grandmother in the 1950s. Black or white, "It didn't matter where you stood," she said. Other information on racial relations in Wilmington are from *Every Man Should Try* by Hubert A. Eaton (Wilmington, N.C.: Bonaparte Press, 1984), pp. 23, 45, 53.

Information about George's employment with Mrs. Pembroke Jones is from telephone interviews with George Evans and C. Reynolds Brown.

Details about how white people treated Minnie are from telephone interviews with Minnie Clauson, Claude Howell, and Jo Kallenborn.

Chapter 4: *The Angel That Stands by Me*

George Evans's description of his mother's emotional crisis is from a telephone interview with the author on May 25, 1994.

Chapter 5: *God Dressed This World in Green*

A brief description of how Mrs. Henry Walters created Airlie Gardens is in *Historic Wilmington—New Hanover County, North Carolina*, ed. Ida Brooks Kellam (Wilmington, N.C.: Stamp Defiance Chapter of the National Society, Daughters of the American Revolution, 1960), p. 30.

Details about Minnie's working conditions at Airlie were gathered from telephone interviews with Jo Kallenborn on May 26, 1994, and George Evans on August 18, 1994.

Impressions of Minnie are from an interview with Jerome McGann on April 7, 1994; an interview with Cecil Lang in July 1994; and telephone interviews with Claude Howell and Ben Williams on August 18, 1994.

Chapter 6: *Beautiful Dreamer*

Information about the career of Nina Howell Starr was taken from her résumé and telephone interviews with the author on August 19 and September 23, 1994.

Nina Starr's description of seeing Minnie Evans's art is from an interview with the author on April 8, 1994.

Nina Starr complained about her exclusion from an exhibit at the Museum of Modern Art in the 1972 issue of *Feminist Art Journal*.

Minnie Evans's quotation "president of my pictures in New York" is from the essay "Minnie Evans: Innocent Surrealist" by Nina Starr in *Minnie Evans: Artist*, ed. Charles Lovell (Greenville, N.C.: East Carolina University, 1993).

Nina Howell Starr's comments on changing the wording of Minnie's title are from telephone interviews with the author on May 13, 1993, and September 19, 1994.

Information about the financial aspect of Minnie's career was gathered from an interview with Nina Starr on April 7, 1994; Nina Starr's comments during the symposium at East Carolina University on May 14, 1993; and a letter from Minnie Evans to Nina Starr dated January 7, 1965.

The unsigned article "Beautiful Dreamer" appeared in *Newsweek* on August 4, 1969. Nina Starr's response appeared in a letter to the editor on September 1, 1969.

Chapter 7: *His Eye Is on the Sparrow*

George Evans described "speaking meetings" in a telephone interview with the author on May 25, 1994.

The quotation "Now we will hear from Minnie Evans" is taken from a telephone interview with Nina Starr on March 28, 1994.

Mechal Sobel's *Trabelin' On: The Slave Journey to an Afro-Baptist Faith* (Princeton, N.J.: Princeton University Press, 1979), pp. 19–20, provided background on black women's participation in African and Afro-Christian religions.

For an essay on possible African influences in southern black art, see the introduction by Judith McWillie to the exhibit catalog *Another Face of the Diamond: Pathways Through the Black Atlantic South* (New York: INTAR Latin American Gallery, 1988). In the same catalog, John Mason mentions Minnie Evans in his essay "Old Africa Anew." Sharon D. Koota discusses Minnie Evans's art in "Cosmograms and Cryptic Writings: 'Africanisms' in the Art of Minnie Evans" in *The Clarion: America's Folk Art Magazine* (Summer 1991).

Alice Rae Yellen talks about the importance of the written word in American folk art in her essay "The Setting: The South," which appears in the exhibit catalog *Passionate Visions of the South: Self-Taught Artists from 1940 to the Present* (Oxford, Miss.: The University Press of Mississippi, 1993).

Chapter 8: *This Is My Heart*

The statement about "anti-art" was made by Claude Howell in a telephone interview with the author on August 18, 1994.

Jo Kallenborn related Minnie's comment about the London exhibit during the symposium at East Carolina University on May 15, 1993.

Minnie's statement "My hand is not as steady now as it was then" and the remark about her "weak knees" are from *The Angel That Stands by Me.*

Jo Kallenborn described the state of Minnie's feet in a telephone interview with the author on May 25, 1994.

Afterword

George Evans related his anecdote about the returned painting during the symposium at East Carolina University on May 15, 1993.

Author's Note

Most of the information for *Painting Dreams* was gathered from taped interviews of Minnie Evans and the recollections of family, friends, and acquaintances. I drew additional facts from a film made about Minnie in 1983.

These oral sources provided a personal glimpse of the artist and her long life. But memories can change or disappear over time. Minnie often gave a different year for the same event, so I have chosen the dates that seem most accurate.

Some details about Minnie's life are unknown, forgotten, or confused in the minds of those who knew her. When I heard conflicting stories from family and friends, I chose the version most likely to be true.

Titles that Minnie gave to her pictures are enclosed within quotation marks. Titles assigned by others are printed in brackets.

Acknowledgments

I am grateful to C. Reynolds Brown, Minnie Clauson, George Evans, Claude Howell, Jo Kallenborn, Cecil Lang, Jerome McGann, Nina Howell Starr, and Ben Williams, who generously shared their memories of Minnie Evans. Andrew Cahan, Berdell Fleming, Ann J. Smith, and Laurel Sneed offered useful insights about photography, religion, and art. Many thanks to the Virginia Foundation for the Humanities and Public Policy for a fellowship that allowed me to complete this book.

DATE DUE

OCT 0 7 2009			

The Library Store   #47-0103